# A Man After Her

# Heart

E L I J A H   J O N E S

**author**HOUSE®

*AuthorHouse™*
*1663 Liberty Drive*
*Bloomington, IN 47403*
*www.authorhouse.com*
*Phone: 833-262-8899*

*Published by AuthorHouse  02/11/2022*

*ISBN: 978-1-6655-5193-9 (sc)*
*ISBN: 978-1-6655-5192-2 (e)*

# Contents

# Black Kryptonite

My love is what I must put on
Display if no words is what I'm left
To say casting my cares upon this poem
In which I now compose about the beauty

Of the women known as the black kryptonite truly its
Wonderful in their design and carefully crafted as if
They were divine and when I think about it I no longer
Think about all my woes when it comes to them being

Black kryptonite because they are the kind of women who's
Worth sliver and gold could never measure truly women
Among women what an incredible treasure and no matter which
Way my life goes ill always love my black kryptonite

Because my love for women like you is
something that I could never
Let fade because I will always value and will forever adore
How you alone were made one of my greatest inspirations you've
Been in helping me write this elegant prose because
Black women you my black kryptonite

# What Feels Right

Love for a beautiful black woman like you wouldn't
Feel right if it was done with all my might
And if you weren't apart of my master plan
Then how could I even call myself a man

And all I need is the pathway to your heart if
You give me a chance because your life I know
I could enhance and whatever it is that you need
I know I can be and to your heart can I hold the key

Because you are what feels right and you are
What makes everything feel all right and these feelings
That I know have did not just come out of the blue
Because they formed overtime from me wanting you

And do not you know that if you need to relax that I can
Be your peace and as for this heart of mine you can have
More than just a piece and I mean everything that I've said
And my talk is not cheap and my love for you runs eternally deep

# Facing Fears

It takes a certain kind of man
To put his heart on his sleeve and on
The line and still hope and pray that everything
Will be fine and it takes a certain kind of man

To say that to the woman that he really loves within
Everything in him to always put her first and never put her
Last or his own heartbreak will break him down fast because
To not put you as my woman first should never be the case

Because you have always been my security and embrace
And there is not a woman like you in this world that id ever
Chase because to me your more than a woman that I know is
So fine and what angel that I know can say is all mine

And days without you in them are days that I live in
Vain and without you being my sunshine there is only
The pouring rain and I can know say all this without shedding
Tears because now I am facing my fears

# In A Man Like Me

In a man like me I will make you
Believe that if true love and affection is
What you desire then that is what you will
Achieve because a woman like you was

Heavenly made and born never to fade
And because you are what allows my heart
To be as open as it is it's never been left the
Same and to take the journey to enter your mind

Is my main aim and with no delay please listen?
To these words in which I now say because I want
To be a man that can be the answer to your cries
And I want to be the man can wipe the tears from

Your eyes because you're all the woman I need in my
Life because without you ill only lose and then feel the
Blues and it is only you that makes this prideful heart of
Mine concede because you are all the
Woman I'll ever need

# Ebony

Ebony when they tell you that your only
Pretty for a dark skin girl tell them that not even all
The diamonds rubies and pearls could ever compare to the
Very beauty that is your very essence as a dark skin
Girl and that your dark skin is more than what some would
Say is just an anomaly and tell them that you could
Never be seen as ugly because ebony your dark
Skin is beautiful and will always be more than amazing because
You are and have always been more than just pretty a dark skin girl
Because God has crafted and molded
you to be more than incredible
And ebony you should never let stereotypes
define who you are as a dark
Skin girl because those who judge you and your skin tone
Don't really know who you are

# Black Women You Are

Black women you are women who should always
Feel loved and respected and
Black women you are women who should never feel
Neglected because a true

Proverbs 31 woman is who you as black women
Have always reflected and
God made you more than enough for any man
You should never feel rejected and

Black women when you hurt, I hurt and when you
I cry because we as black people are all connected
And to you is where all my time love and attention
Has and will always be directed and black women

I want to do everything in my power to put you first as is
Expected and you will always be the women whom
I as a black man have forever selected and anything that
I can do I will because never leave you feeling alone or

Unprotected

# Ebony pt 2

And some people can't seem to understand and want themselves
And ebony you are more what some people would
Say Is short and nappy hair and you are more than just a
Dark skin girl full of anger and ebony your beauty
And your grace and who you are as a dark skin

Girl is equal to any other light skinned girl so
how could they ever be more Superior to you as
A dark-skinned girl and again you are a beautiful dark
Skin Girl and you should never let the haters and naysayers

Get you down because ebony you were never
Ugly and now you know the value of your
Worth and how it was never defined by the words in which
Others say and light skinned girls where never better than

You because light skinned girls because all black women
Are beautiful in their own special way and someone's
Personal perception of one's complexion could never
Determine your beauty as dark and light skinned women

# Black Women You Are Pt 2

And black women in the beauty and grace is what
God himself has fully perfected
And to that statement alone it doesn't even
Matter who or what has objected

To all that I have said because black women
It is your lives and beings being affected
And all the hurt pain and woe that black
Men and American society throws has been

Detected but black women keep your head up
High and never be deceived by what can be injected
By those who only want to see you fall and fail and leave
You lost in the cold and left so dejected and the hurtful

Statements and actions that come to attack you as
Women needs to be corrected

# My Better Half

This poem goes out to my melanin queens
Whose melanin wonders and being reign supreme
In all things and every way and it is those melanin wonders
That will never go and will forever stay because my melanin

Queens you are my better half and I love you even more
For it You are the woman for me and just want to be
The only man for you because I love my dark skin
Queens and my light skin queens because the all the

Power honor and glory belongs to you and to all the
Melanin queens with melanin rich dark chocolate
Brown skin never wash it away it is what I need as a
Black man and every day of my life I hunger and thirst

And fiend for it because like India Aire and
Musiq soul child I to need reach my chocolate highs
And that chocolate high can only come from
Beautiful melanin queens like you that radiate

Your melanin wonders like angels' wings because
Melanin queens your more than heavenly
And that is why you are and
Will always be my better half

# For Your Love

Black women as a black man I will die for your love
And embrace and black women for your love I will do
Whatever it takes just to be in the mist of your grace and
Black women for your love my heart that is open for you
Continues in this lover's race and black women

You are what no other woman could ever be nor ever replace
And black women you will always be my happily
Ever after but I am no case and black women for
Your love I will always look toward your secret place

And black women for your love I will continue to seek
Your face and black women how I feel for your love
Nothing in this world could ever erase and black women
For your love I will be the kind of man who can be concrete

And black women for your love I can be the kind
Of man who can be complete and black women for your
Love I can be the man who is devoted only to you
And never cheat and black women for your love it will

Never be you who I as a man would ever mistreat
And black women for your love I
Could never come at you with deception and deceit
And black women for your love my heart realizes

That you are what makes it beat

# Beautiful To Me

Black women just too beautiful for me as a man not to
See you as majesty truly my everything irreplaceable
Love of my life and the light that comes from you and
Only shines in the mist of my darkest of days and more
Then amazing Is what you are to me and until the end of

Time you will always be my one and only love black women
Because black women you truly are special to me and my
Eyes will forever be on you because your just to beautiful
For a man like me to not love care for and cherish for all time

And I thought that this was something that you needed to know
And this was always something that I as a black man needed
To show and from my heart to your heart my love for you
Continues to grow as these happy tears of love and joy

Begin to flow and I will continue to love and hold onto to
You more than you will ever know
Because you are beautiful just too beautiful for me as a man
To see you any other way black women

# Chocolate Girls

Chocolate girls I've never meet such beautiful brown
Skin girls quite like you Who could be who you are and
Do what you as brown skin girls do? and I never knew
That being around brown skin chocolate girls could feel

So right And I never knew that I would want to love them
With all my might chocolate girls you are my everything
And all of who you are as chocolate girls is what you always
Bring and I love how you make me feel as though I am a

Black king and in your love, I will always be wrapped up in
Like an angel's wing and for the love of you chocolate girls
I will now and forever fight because it is this flame in this
Heart of mine in which you as chocolate girls ignite

And so, I hold you close to me because I need to be
In your embrace so damn tight because chocolate
Girls you are my strength my love life and my light
And in these brown eyes of mine of my you as

Beautiful brown skin chocolate girls will always
Shine and I just need for you as brown skin chocolate
Girls to stay in my life and be all mine

# Chocolate Girls Pt 2

And brown skin chocolate girls you are the greatest being
that I could ever view in sight And I know that if you are in my
life everything in this life of mine will be all right
And when things in my life feel like its growing dim you

Make my life feel bright again and I love how you always
Been there for me and have always come to my rescue
And I loved the fact that you kept it real especially when
Everyone was being fake but not you because you've always

Been there right by side more than a friend could ever be
And that's true and brown skin chocolate girls
I know that you will always be around
Until we both are over and through

# Black Cocoa Girls

Black cocoa girls are what I'd give the world up just so
they would be mine and black cocoa girls are the girls that
I want to see more than win I want to see them shine
And black cocoa girls were blessed to
have such dark chocolate skin

So lovely and divine and black cocoa girls were beautifully
And wonderfully made in god's image and design
And black cocoa girls more than what I need and will now
And forever be my everything and black cocoa girls have all

Of what makes them beautiful black queens to bring
To the table and black cocoa girls are the very reason why
I as a black man can truly sing and the thought of not have you
Black cocoa girls in my life would more than just sting

Because black cocoa girls you are
The reason why
I as a black man love and
Am able to write

# Black Cocoa Girls Pt 2

And black cocoa girls you are the reason why I even
Have words to say and even recite
And black cocoa girls your chocolate and very beings
Will always be beautiful in my sight

And through my darkest of days on this earth
Black cocoa girls you have always been my light
And black cocoa girls for you I do anything and
Until time stands till, I'll always be right here

And with each statement that I make in my poems
I just want my point to be clear
Because black cocoa girls I truly hold your heart love
And everything about you oh so dear

And black cocoa girls you should know that I as a
Black man won't just up and disappear
And black cocoa girls you are the only girls
That I as a black man will treasure and forever admire

Because black cocoa girls I see the beauty of your
Brown skin and its value that I truly desire
And black cocoa girls when life left me alone and
Burnt out you because my endless fire

And to be the black man that you as black
Cocoa girls need for me to be is what you require
Her Beautiful Wonders

I love Leah Gordone and all her
Beautiful wonders and how my very
Thoughts of her and all of her beauty and

Ways echoes and thunders because Leah I love
The way woman like you was made to shine
And I as a man only wish that you were

Mine because I love you because you are
A strong woman and queen who has lost many
Things and has faced many things and this is
Why I as a black man and as a human being

Have embraced each and every little thing about
You because you're the only type of woman at
This point in my life that I as a man truly want to have
And to love and to forever pursue because your more
Beautiful than anything ever known and your
More beautiful than any racial stone because the price

For a love like yours and yours alone has already been paid
For your very beautiful and precious
Melanin tone and for your very bone and this is why
I will always and forever continue to
Honor you and Leah you are the definition of
A black woman and this what you have always
Shown with all of your wonders

# You Mean The World To Me

Black women you mean the world to someone like me
And black women only you alone can set this broken heart
And mind of mine free and black women you have always
Opened your arms of love and embrace so wide

Even when I hurt and disrespected you whether in my words
And actions misguided in pride And I want to apologize
For not always putting you as black women first
Because know I understand that when you give and do not get

Back that feeling is the worst and again, black women you mean
The world to someone like me and black women only you
Alone can set this broken heart and mind of mind free
And black women wherever you are I know that your

Love is not too far away and black women I know that
When I am around you my day becomes an even brighter day
And black women I could never imagine even living a day
Without you because my life would not be the same

Without you

# You Mean The World To Me Pt 2

And black women you are more than wonder and more
Then amazing and you are the only women that I as a
Man should ever be praising
Because when I felt so lost and alone black women you

Sparked within me a new flame
And in you as black women I being a black man
Should do the same

And again, black women you have always opened your
Arms of love and embrace so wide even when I hurt and
Disrespected you whether in my words and actions
Misguided in pride and black women I love the way that your

Chocolate skin radiates and shines
And I love how I as a black man am all yours and how you
As black women are all mines

# True Love Does Not Die

Black woman the feelings that I have for you as a black
Man is something that I as a black man could never deny
Because true love does not lie even when I was that prodigal
Negro chasing After other females that could never be you,

The fact remains that true love does not lie and it kills me
To say this but black woman can you please restore my lost
Honor that i lost in All my racial pride and black woman can
You fix my broken road so that I as a broken black man

Can find my way back to you because I know that I've
Caused a lot of hurt and have said a lot of things that I
Cannot take back so I come before you in genuine
Humility and ask and hope and pray that you can forgive

Me because I was a foolish man who spoke without wisdom
And understanding and now I know the error of my ways So
Can you please help me find your grace and majesty so that I can?
Love on you and need and want you like I should have because

I was the ungrateful negro and I'll admit that because
Again, true love does not lie so again can you give this
Broken black man another tries because I'm pouring out my love
Like I should have done but did not do and for that again sorry

# And I Say This From My Heart

Black women I truly treasure honor and adore your
Very beings and I say this from my heart because black
Women you need to know that by me you will always be
Loved and appreciated and black women I know you have

Always been there for me from the very start of my
Very being as a black man and therefore from you I
Could never grow apart Because black women my feelings
For you must be more than what can be reciprocated Black

Women I truly treasure honor and adore your very beings
And I say this from my heart and it is to you as black women
To whom I as a black man go to pursue when I dart
Towards your direction because your chocolate highs

And melanin radiance leaves me captivated and black
Women I know you have always been there for me
From the very start and your love is so sweet and could
Never in this lifetime or the next be tart Because black love

Black beauty and black women are the best things god has
Ever created black women I truly treasure honor and adore
Your very beings and I say this from my heart
And black women you are the definition of that song when it

# And I Say This From The Heart Continued

Talked about the best part because it has always been you and
Always will be you and this will always go undebated
And black women I know you have always been there for me
From the very start and if I ever said that I didn't love and care

For you that would be a judgment that's not very smart because
Black women I must put you first because when I don't it makes
Things so complicated black women I truly treasure honor and
Adore your very beings and I say this from my heart and black

Women I know you have always been there for me
From the very start

# My Worst Fear

Look my worst fear is to not have black woman
Here in my life and my worst fear is to see black woman
Disappear and fade away from my good view and my
Worst fear is not having a black woman to have and

To hold dear and my worst fear is when saying all of this
That I was not clear and my worst fear is leaving a black woman
Feeling neglected and my worst fear is leaving a black woman
Feeling unprotected and disrespected because I love black woman

Too much to leave their side and I love black woman too much to
Ignore all the pain that they have gone there and all of the tears that
They have cried and that Is why I will never
leave a black woman denied
Because any and all actions against black
woman could never be justified

And black woman you are to be adored and
magnified and glorified in all the
Beauty grace and style that is and will always
be you because you are black
Woman magic and brown skin wonders and
that will always be more than enough
For me until my time on this earth ends because black woman

Only you can leave me satisfied

# Everything That I Have In Me

Look black women I just want you to know that everything
That I have in me I will provide because black women I know
That you need the kind of man who can come to your aid
And I would not let anything in this world come between

Us not even my own pride because anything that keeps you as
Black women from being happy, I will put to the side
Because nothing in this world comes before you and I refuse
To every see you as women ever fade look black women I just

Want you to know that everything that I have in me I will provide
And black women I know that I can be the man that need in your
Life to help and to guide you away-from all the hurt and all the pain
And all those so-called men who left you
betrayed and I would not let

Anything in this world come between us not even my own pride
And the arms of all this love that I have to you as black women
Are all open wide and no, I am not like those other men and I
Promise you I will never leave you feeling played and black women

I just want you to know that everything
that I have in me will provide
And since I am so open and ready from the door all I need to know
Is if your down to ride with me and for me
because being your protection
And selection is all I have conveyed and
I would not let anything in this

World come between us not even my own
pride and I want you to know
That any need that you have I will do more than have it supplied

And black women when you with a man
like me you will never again
Feel alone or afraid look black women I just
want you to know that everything

That I have me will provide and I would
not let anything in this world
Come between us not even my own pride

# You Mean The World To Me Pt 2

Black woman you have and will always mean the world to me
And you're always on my mind because black woman you are more
Then incredible and you are and have always been more than
Wonderful To have in this life of mine truly incomparable to

Any other woman or being that god could have ever made
And I'll tell you why it's because you mean the world to me
And so ill forever put you first above any and all woman because
No other woman is quite like you and no other woman can do

What you can do and no other woman has that melanin wonder
And glory that is so godlike and divine and no other woman could
Have that chocolate glowing radiance
and shine and no other woman
Could ever hope would be mine because
black woman you mean this

Whole world to me and I wouldn't trade
You for anyone or anything because
Your irreplaceable in every way

# What My Love Can Provide

Black women don't you know that I can be whatever you need
With what my love can provide and all I really need is for you
As black women to give a man like me a chance because black
Women you will always have a friend in
me with loving arms open wide

And black women I want you to know that
I can put an end to all the tears
In which you have cried because I will
always be there no matter what is
Going on in your circumstance black women
don't you know that I can be
Whatever you need with what my love can
provide and the one thing that

You will never have to worry about is my
pride and I won't allow for it to
Hold me back especially when I want you as
women to advance because black
Women you will always have a friend in
me with loving arms open wide
Because I love you and I care for you and
I will make sure that every need

That you have is supplied and black women
because of who you are this will
Always be my personal viewpoint and stance
black women don't you know
That I can be whatever you need with what
my love can provide and everything
That I say about you as black women I say with purpose and stride

And all want to do is lift you up in love because it is your life that I
Want to enhance because black women
you win always have a friend
In me with loving arms open wide and
until this very life of mine ends
I will always be by your side and every time
I think about you as beautiful

Black women, I fall into this chocolate high of a trance
Black women don't you know that I can be whatever you need
With what my love can provide because black women you will
Always have a friend in me with loving arms open wide

# *Before Anyone Else*

Black women you have and will always come
Before anyone else because you are the definition
Of B.A.E and you will always be before anyone else
And no other woman will come before because all past

Mentions of any other woman before you have always
Passed away in the many fleeting memories of time because
Putting another woman before you is a reality that I as a
Black man could never again face because words were

Said and mistakes were made and I hope that in these words
Of mine that the price of my once sinful words and actions
Can be paid because those other women and my thoughts of
Them are over and dead and I no longer want to relive that chapter

So, I closed the chapter of that so called
book and left behind the ways of
Myoid transgressions because what I said
should have said should have
Never been said and what I've done should
have never been done and
That is why this poem of mine is called
bae because the woman that

I called bae should have never been called
bae because black women
I finally realized that I should have never put anyone else
Before you black women and I promise you
that I will never do that again
Because my loyalty and devotion to you black women is undivided

And as for my once sinful
Words and actions and I will never again
Allow myself to be so caught up other females
And end up misguided again

*No Interruptions*

Black women I just want to love and
embrace you with no interruptions
Or complications because as a black man
who loves black women, I just
Have so much love for you to share and I
refuse to not uplift and encourage
You because you deserve my all with no
hesitations and my love poems about

You are more than just some mere poetic
driven declaration's because it is a
True pleasure just to be around and no
other feeling could ever compare
Black women I just want to love and
embrace you with no interruptions
Or complications and black women you
are the most beautiful and lovely

Beings out of all god creations because
there is no other woman quite
Like you with such chocolate brown skin,
I swear and I refuse too not
Uplift and encourage you because you
deserve my all with no hesitations
Because black women you have always
and will always defy any and all

Expectations of who and what people expect
and think that a black woman
Should be and you shouldn't care black
women I just want to love and

Embrace you with no interruptions or
complications and black women
I hope that my love poems honor you and
your legacies from all generations

And I also hope that my love poems can help
lead you out of your heartaches
And despair and I refuse to not uplift and
encourage you because you deserve
My all with no hesitations and I want to
be that kind of man who can
Bring new life to each one of your aspirations
because I want for my love

Poems to take on what you as black women feel like you can't bare
Black women I just want to love and embrace you with
No interruptions or complications and I refuse to not uplift
And encourage you because you deserve my all with no hesitations

# Open From The Door

Look black women all I need for you to
know is that my love for is you was
Open from the door and that will not ever
change because you are and will
Always be so incredible to me and of your
dark rich melanin driven skin and
Its wonders all I want is more because I fiend
for you like caffeine and it will

Always be my love for you that I pour out
to you because you are everything
That I could ever want or need for you to be
look black women all I need for
You to know is that my love for you was open
from the door and you will always
Be the kind of women that I give the praise
and honor to because I adore

You because black women you are more
than my words could say and
You have set this heart of mine free and of
your dark rich melanin driven skin
And its wonders all I want is more because
black women you have allowed for
My heart to take flight and do more than soar
into the presence and peace that

Only can be found within you from what
these brown eyes of mine can see
Look black women all I need for you to
know is that my love for you was

Open from the door and I mean what I say
from of the bottom of this very
Heart of mine and the very core of who I as
a man because the best of who I am

I will always give I grantee and of your dark
rich melanin driven skin and its
Wonders all I want is more and black women
I will be what no other man was
For you like never before because you hold me
by the heart and to everything that
I have and run you hold the key look black
women all I need for you to know

Is that my love for you was open from the door?
And of your dark rich melanin driven skin and its
Wonders all I want is more

# There Will Never Be

Black women there will truly never be someone like you because
Who and what you are is what no other
woman can be and I am saying?
This sincerely and as open and honest as I
can be so you know that its true
And all the love that I have for you will
never fall through because you

Exactly what you mean to me black women
there will truly never be someone
Like you and every day that you live and draw
breath makes my life feel so brand new
Because I appreciate you and the very air
that you breathe with so much glee
And I'm saying this sincerely as open and honest
as I can be so you know that its true

And as time went on more and more of my
feelings and inner emotions for you grew
And for you I cry and for you I as a real man
will get down on bended knee
Black women there will truly never be
someone like you and black women
You were made for me to love and to pursue and
in this life, of mine you will be forever

Planted like an apple tree and I'm saying this sincerely and as open
And honest as I can be so you know that
its true and black women you

Will always be the one thing that I must
view because to this heart and life
Of mine you hold the master key black women there will truly

Never be someone like you and I'm saying this sincerely
And as open and honest as I can be so
You know that its true

# I Have To Be That Man

Oh, black women I have to be that man who would
Never cheat and I have to be that man who makes
You feel oh so complete and I have to be that man
Who's love for you and you being is forever sweet

And I have to be that man who doesn't have to hold
Onto his pride and I have to be the kind of man
Who has women like you on my side and I have to be that?
Man, who can be everything that you need for me to be and

I need to be that man that puts no other woman above you if
I as a real man say that I love you and I have to be that man
Who can be the kind of man after your heart and I have to be?
That man who would never part from your life if I say that you

Mean everything to me and you do not have to be Monica
But black women you know that your mean everything to me
And more and that is the man that I have to be for you because
I adore you and I truly love and care for you and with everything

In my being I will live up to my words and openly confess how
I truly feel about you because I just have to be that man because
If that man isn't me another man will end up taking my place
And I won't allow that to be the case

# Believe In Me

Black women you are loved and you are worthy and you can always
Lean on and believe in me because love
for you is strong and it refuses
To ever waver and whatever you need me
I'm there and because of who
I am as a man just know that when I give, I give my all unto to thee

And black women you will always be
honored praised and adored because
Your worthy and I know that there are black
women that need to this and this
Will always be what I share black women
you are loved and you are worthy
And you can always lean on and believe in
me and black women you are truly

The most beautiful women that these brown
eyes of mine can see and there
Will never come a day when this will not
be what I as a black man declare
And because of who I am as a man just know
that when I give, I give my all
Unto to thee and black women don't you
know that you are the greatest beings

Ever made by the lord god almighty and that you can always trust
And depend on me and that is on my life
I solemnly swear black women
You are loved and you are worthy and you
can always lean on and believe in me
And no matter what happens my dedication
and appreciation for you is what I

Will always guarantee because when I said
that I loved and would put you
First is what I meant because I truly care
and because of who I am as a man
Just know that when I give, I give my all unto
to thee and I'll continue to convey
This and say this even while crying out like
jodeci and boyz to men on bended

Knee because black women no matter what
you go through all of who you
Are is what will always bare black women
you are loved and you are worthy and
You can always lean on and believe in me
and because of who I am as a
Man, just know that when I give, I give my all unto to thee

# The Way That I Love You

Black women there is not a man in this whole world that I say what
I say and do what I do and most importantly
there is not a man in this
World who could ever love you the way
that I do because black women
My love for you has never been misplaced
and black women you see that

My for you love is true and that I will always
love you and you will always
Be the greatest being and treasure that my
being could ever view and I will
Always embrace you and I will always chase
you and I will never let you go
Because I want you more than I want to
breathe and I want you more than I

Want to see and in this life of mine is right
where I need for you to be because
No other man could ever love touch and hold
you like I can and no other man
Could ever worship cherish praise and adore
you like I can because no other man
Could ever hold your heart in his hand like I
do and no other man could ever give

His undivided love and attention to you
quite like I can because no other
Man will ever understand the way that I love
you like I do and no other man
Will fiend for you and crave you the way that
I do and no other man could make

You his everything the way that I do and no
other man could make you the only

Women that he will ever pursue like I can and
will always do and I am saying this
Sincerely and as open and honest as I can be
so you know that its true and all the
Love that I have for you will never fall through
because you exactly what you mean
To me black women there will truly never be
someone like you and every day that
You live and draw breath makes my life feel so
Brand new because I appreciate you

# The Way That I Love You Pt 2

And the very air that you breathe with so
much glee And I'm saying this
Sincerely as open and honest as I can be so
you know that its true and as time
Went on more and more of my feelings
and inner emotions for you grew
And for you I cry and for you I as a real man
will get down on bended knee

Black women there will truly never be
someone like you and black women
You were made for me to love and to pursue
and in this life, of mine you will
Be forever planted like an apple tree and I'm
saying this sincerely and as open
And honest as I can be so you know that its
true and black women you will always

Be the one thing that I must view because to this heart and
Life of mine you hold the master key black women there will
Truly never be someone like you and I'm saying this sincerely and
As open and honest as I can be so you know that its true

# I Have To Be That Man

Oh, black women I have to be that man who would never cheat
And I have to be that man who makes you feel oh so complete and
I have to be that man Who's love for you
and you being is forever sweet
And I have to be that man who doesn't
have to hold onto his pride and I

Have to be the kind of man who has women
like you on my side and I have
To be that man who can be everything that
you need for me to be and I need
To be that man that puts no other woman
above you if I as a real man say that
I love you and I have to be that man who can
be the kind of man after your heart

And I have to be that man who would never part
from your life if I say that you mean
Everything To me and you do not have to be Monica
but black women you know that your
Mean everything to me and more and that is the
man that I have to be for you because I adore
You and I truly love and care for you and with
everything in my being I will live up

To my words and openly confess how I truly feel
About you because I just have to be that man
Because if that man isn't me another man will end up
Taking my place and I won't allow that to be the case

# Left Incomplete

To each melanin queen that could ever exist this world this very
Poem and all its words are for you and for your eyes only because
Black women you are the light that makes my day and when I'm
Around you make me feel like everything is going to be okay

And the love that I have for you I can feel in my soul and when
I feel like my life is in pieces you make me feel whole again and
These some of the many things that I could never be discrete about
Because all my heart has been open like
an emotional door and of your

Being black women, I Just want more
because without your love and your
Being so sweet I would just feel so incomplete
and there is not a day that
Goes by that I won't cry for you and you
alone and there's not a day that
I won't cry for you and you alone because
when I said that you where my

Everything that Is exactly what I meant
because to me you where heaven
Sent and, in my past, I may have chased
after girls who were not you
But those days are over because I realize
that those girls could never
Compete with you because those girls could never be you and again

Without your love and your love alone, I would feel so incomplete

# When God Gave You To Me

To all my black women worldwide when God gave you to me,
I knew that he blessed that day because I'm more than fortunate to
Have you in my world and every other woman is who you outshine
And everyone in heaven and on earth knows just how beautiful and

Worthy your day Is and was molded and
made to be along with all its
Endless power and glory always on full
display and that is why everything
In me as a black man wants to make you
all mine to all my black women
Worldwide when God gave you to me, I
knew that he blessed that day

Because God knew that I needed you here in my life to forever stay
And black women what where and who
would I be without you if God
Had not given me you as my sign and
everyone in heaven and on earth
Knows just how beautiful and worthy your
clay Is to me because black

Women you are have always been my
personal gateway and all I want
To be is forever be attached to you and all
your endless love just like a vine
To all my black women world-wide when
God gave you to me, I knew that
He blessed that day and until I have run out
of words to use my love and devotion

To you is what I will always convey and
black women I will never be the
Kind of man that would ever cross you or
the line and everyone in heaven
And on earth knows just how beautiful and
worthy your clay Is and what it means
To me and all I am saying all of this with no
delay and nothing could ever make

You fall from heaven because you were made divine to all my
Black women worldwide when God gave you to me, I knew that
He blessed that day and everyone in heaven and on earth knows
Just how beautiful and worthy your clay

# Whatever You Want In A Man

Look black women whatever you want
in a man I will be without any
Debate and this is promise to always be
there for you and this is what I will
Forever declare because I now know and
understand the power of black love and
What it can create and all the love and words
that I say about you as beautiful black

Women just could not wait because
whatever is on my heart and mind
Concerning my black queens is what I
need to share and black women
Whatever you want in a man I will be
without any debate and if you need
Some love and trust and commitment then
being with a man like me is fate

Because black women I love and appreciate who you are
And what you do and all that you bare because I now know
And understand the power of black love and what it can create
And I'm going to continue to tell you
just how much I love and need

You and I will not hesitate because I will always be here for you
And you can place your hurt and pain in my care and black women
Whatever you want in a man I will be without any debate
And for the sake of who you are as black women I will forever

Advocate For you because as I long as I
long to be a man after your heart I

Refuse to see you in despair because I
now know and understand the
Power of black love and what It can create
and never again will I put any
Other women before you since I am setting the record straight

Because black women I only want to be around you as I appreciate
Breathing your very air and black women
whatever you want in a man
I will be without any debate because I now know and understand
The power of black love and what it can truly create

# Love You More

To all my beautiful black queens
I as a black man want to be your open door
And I as a black man want to be your something more
Because my melanin queens you mean more than this whole

World to me and everything in me as a black man wants only
You and longs for only you because when I am around beautiful
Black queens like you I no longer feel like
I am alone and I when I am
Around you I feel like I can soar and truly walk into the realties

Of forevermore and I mean all what I have said because my black
Queens I need your loving and embrace
from the bottom of my core
And that is all I want to feel from you
because all I want to do is love
You more and when I'm around you I feel
like there are greater things

In store because my beautiful black queens
I as a black man want to give
You all of me because open is the doors
of my heart with all emotions
And introspective lines of verse and you beautiful black queens are
The most beautiful women that I have ever
known and your complexion

And chocolate wonders are greater than
what any other female could
Have shown and I all want is the love that
you beautiful black queens

Alone give and again, I thank you for you
being the beautiful black queens
And the women that God has allowed for
you to be and until time stands still
I'll always love you more

# Beautiful Brown Eyes

Oh, brown skin girls do not you know that I love you and
your beautiful brown eyes and I love the way that they look because
They truly amazing when they shine and
when I look into your eyes,
I begin to truly see the heaven's bright
skies and all the love that I have

For them I promise you that will be the one thing that I will never
Comprise because brown skin girls your
beautiful brown eyes are truly
Unmatched in design oh, brown skin girls
do not you know that I love you
And your beautiful brown eyes and when I
look into your beautiful brown eyes

All I can see is me caught up in endless highs because brown skin
Girls you are and will always be so incredible to me and oh so fine
To see and when I look into your eyes, I
begin to truly see the heaven's
Bright skies and brown skin girls I want you to know that my

Love for you is eternally yours because it never dies and beautiful
Incredible and amazing is what you as women
are and what you will always
Define oh, brown skin girls do not you know
that I love you and your beautiful
Brown eyes and brown skin girls I want you
to know that you are the only reason

Why I can even rise because as a man I
give you all my heart because

I am always yours and your all mine and when
I look into your eyes, I begin too truly
See the heaven's bright skies and every bit
of feeling and emotion that I have
For you brown skin girls I will do more than
just treasure when I begin to vocalize

# You Make Me So Happy

Black women you make me so happy and I'm
So, in awe of you that I stand amazed I that I must confess
That you leave me so mesmerized by all the beautiful
Wonders that lies in beautiful black women like you

And all the love that I have for you is what I will never in this
Lifetime second guess and I'm so happy that God allowed for you
To come into my life and that it was my
life that he chose to bless me
With you because black women you are
truly the greatest blessing that

God could have ever allowed for me as a
black man to have hold and forever
View black women you make me so happy
and I am so in awe of you that I stand
Amazed that I must confess that you as black
women are and will always be my
Dreams come true and all the love that I have
for you is what I will never in this

Lifetime second guess and to a man like me holding your heart in
My hands I hope that the answer will be yes because black women
You are so incredible and I need your love like the heaven needs
Its dew

# Feelings

Now as a man my own feelings can go
Even deeper than a drake or Ella Mai song
And my feelings can show how I truly feel
About the kind of girl that I want and love that

I mean what I say, and I say just what I mean because
Putting my heart out there for the girl that I as a man
Love and care for could never be wrong because in that
Special girls' heart is where I as a man feel as though I belong

And I feel as though this is way that it should have been
All along because if I ever say that I love you and have
Always had love for you then that is what I meant and if I
Say that you mean everything to me as a man then I will

Make that more that more than evident because only
A girl like you so deep in these feelings of mine
That I hope and pray some beautiful girl will truly see
And allow for them to all shine for her and her alone.

# So Many Butterflies

And in this world and heart of mine there
Is no love that could ever be as sweet as your
Love and there is no other love that could be
As complete as your love and your love alone

Because in my life you are more than concrete
And you make me so happy as a man that my heart
Feels like it could only beat for you because my love
For you never dies and you are the love that is and has

Always been the answer to all my cries and make
Me as a man feel as though I could forever rise into
The eternal mist of cloud nine's memorizing skies
And endless highs because baby only you can fill this

Stomach of mine with so many butterflies
On the inside of who I am, and I have so much
More love for you because of it because I truly
Never felt this way about love until I met you

Ebony your precious melanin darkness could
Ever be matched or even debated

# So Many Butterflies Pt 2

And ebony when I talk about how beautiful
and incredible you are, I
Never once hesitated and ebony I just want to see you as a
Black woman to rise up and forever shine
and ebony just looking into
Your brown skin and eyes makes me want you to be all mine

And ebony you as a black woman are more than what any other
Woman could ever be and ebony your brown skin and brown eyes
Are even more beauty and amazing to see
and ebony the greatest complexion?
That god himself has ever made lies upon on your very bones

Because ebony blessed was your skin
and all its rich features beyond
All other skin tones and ebony ever since
you came into my life it has
Truly never been the same and ebony I
love and appreciate how you've
Given me someone to love and sparked a
new flame and ebony III always

Love you with such an incredible dedication
passion and fire and ebony you
Will always be the woman that I will always
love and desire and ebony you
Will now and forever be the kind of woman
for me and that is more than evident
Because ebony your whole being feels like it
been truly heaven sent and ebony

I will always come to you for love and embrace because I need
Those personal conversations and open letters but I am no case and
Ebony, you give me a reason to put these words onto this very
Paper as I begin to write

# For All Eternity

To my future baby girl this poem like
Many others is all for you baby you truly
Are the love of my life and this light of mine?
I as a man just want to share my love with and for
You for eternity and I just want to sing and dance
At the very thoughts of who you are as a woman and
What you mean to me and all your endless majesty because
The beautiful being in whom God has created you to be is truly
More than wonderful and with this love that I have for you
I will more than declare all the love and feelings that I as
A man have for you as I move toward you because where you
Are baby is where I as a man want and must be because
If I did not have you and only you then who would I as have if the
Woman Is not you for all eternity because no other woman in
All of creation could ever mean what you as a woman mean to me

# A Virtuous Woman

A virtuous woman is a black woman
Whos' price is far above rubies and a virtuous woman
Is a black woman who always stays on your mind
And a virtuous woman is a black woman is love
Kind and true and has always waited on someone
Like me and you and a virtuous woman is a black
Woman who in my eyes will always shine
And a virtuous woman is a black woman
Is just so chocolate fine and a virtuous woman is a
Black woman who should always be put first
Whether she is at her best or her worst
And a virtuous woman is a black woman
Who will always complete me and be my everything?
And a virtuous woman is a black woman
Who will always be treated like a queen?
And a virtuous woman is a black woman
Whom I would someday give a wedding ring
Because a black woman is
A virtuous woman

# The Heart Wants What It Wants

If the heart wants what it wants then
Black women my heart wants you
Because I love and care for you and will
always be there for you
And all I want to do is what is best
F or you because I am just that kind
Of man and my life without
You in it is just not worth living again
Black women my heart wants what it
Wants and it wants you right here
With me forever and ever and everything
That I have to give I give it all to you
Because black women my heart mind
Spirit and being all belong to
You

# My Heart Wants You

Oh, black women my heart wants you because
Your so chocolate fine and black women my heart wants
For you to be all mine and black women my heart wants
You in my life to stay and my heart wants you to know
That with a man like me everything will be okay and my heart
Wants you to know that it will never be your heart
That I would ever leave played and my heart wants you to know
That I will never leave you betrayed and my heart wants
You to know that it all belongs to you
Because black women you are my forever ladies
And to one of you out there I want to give you
My babies and black women my heart wants you
To know that you have and always will always meet more
Then meet all my wants and needs and my heart wants
You to know that your love and your heart alone feeds my very soul
And that is what my heart wants for you as
Black women to know

# From Feeling To Being

I am tired of talking about feeling like I want
To be in love instead of being in love
And I just want to go from feeling in love to being
In love now I am not bashing the confession of feelings
But I need more than just some confessions when
My heart love and everything is more than qualified
To have someone to have and to hold and to forever
Love and embrace and to fill this void in this life of
Mine that I call an empty space that no other female could
Fill accept that special female who could be more than my
Anything and everything because a man needs love to and to
Escape this reality of putting so many feelings and emotions
Out there when I feel like no one could possibly love me or
Even begin to and understand who I am and all the love that
I'd be willing to do if just had the chance to go from feeling to
Being in love and this is where this
Poem and its words end

# I Only Have Eyes For You

To the woman who my heart belongs that I call bae
In the core of my heart is where you will forever stay
Because you are my light and radiant sunshine
And with every beat of this heart of mine
I need to make you all mine
And I want to make this more than evident
That I love you and how our time together will forever be spent
And how my love for you has grew
Because I only have eyes for you
Because my feelings for you is what I
will never be afraid to declare
Because in depths of my inner being and
emotions lies the love that I
Must share with you and you alone always
Because you make me a better man and you shine your light in the
Mist of my darkest of days
And you give me so much happiness
And to being with you forever the answer will always be yes
And this what I had to make oh so clear
Because bae I hold you and your heart oh so dear

# Doing It Wrong

And in that one girl's special life
I as a man just want to feel like I truly
Belong and since the feeling of wanting and
Needing of truly being in love continues to be
The case because the way I express confess and
Then address my feelings towards the females that I
Like is something that I am doing wrong and with so
Many things to say and convey about having me a bae
I still end up feeling so lonely on any given day when all
I have ever wanted and needed as a man was someone to call
My own because I hate sleeping alone and being alone and
Again, maybe me putting my feelings and emotions and
Everything that I must give Is just me doing the kind of
Of like singers expressing their emotions at the wrong end
Of a love song and if had to be someone then I guess that
Someone would be a man like me just doing it all wrong

# Love Is Complicated

There has always been love at the very
Core of each and every poem and word
That I have ever uttered and stated and when
It comes down to the one that you love it had
Hit me like the lyrics in that one Avril Lavigne
Song complicated and I want to know why do you
Females have gone and make things so complicated
When I have poured out my heart and all my love to you
And still, what comes from it all is of no real concern
To you and so I feel the flame of what could have been
But I am no Bryson tiller but still I feel the burn because
The love that comes from out of my soul and still I feel
No return and still to this very day wonder why love
Is so damn complicated for me to have as my own and
Still for her love the realities of having everything revealed
Would be more than shown and still I as a man wonder why
Love is so complicated when I've made every feeling and
Emotion that I've ever had

# The Love That I Have For You

Look there's something that I want you to
Understand and I want you to know that any
Thing that I say is all true and that my love for
You is what I as a man could never leave misplaced
Because the love that I have for you means everything
To a man like me and that a forever thing because
I am the kind of man who will give you all the praise
And the honor and the glory whether your right or wrong
And even when your sad I can be the kind of man who
Can make you happy because I'm the man who can truly
Share all of this love in this heart of mine forever and ever
Continue to declare this forever and ever because all of the love
That I have for you isn't going away because it here to stay
Because I love you to do and have things done your way
Because at the end the day you and your heart will have the final
Say and I as a man pray that you don't ever push me and all the love
That I have for you away

# *Faithful*

Look I am more than faithful when
It comes to making you my one and only
Forever lady and I've been faithful enough as a man
To say that you truly are and will always be the only
One for me and everything that you are as a woman
Is exactly what I need as a man and my feelings for
You are all I as a man will forever be expressing and
My love for you and all that god himself has called and
Made you to be is all that I as a man will forever be
Professing faithfully because I want you to know that
You are and will always mean everything to me because
You're such a blessing and with all of this being said there is
No second guessing this for a man like
me because if there ever came
a time when you walked out of my life I as a man would be forever
Stressing and as a faithful man I am and will always be devoted
To you because all I've ever wanted to do was what I as a man have
Seen other lovers do because I didn't want feel as if I
Was all on my own sad and alone but that was until I found you
Because I remained faithful in pursuing what my heart mind
Soul and being had always wanted and that was you

# Putting Myself Out There

Look I as a man have so many feelings
And emotions that I more than want to share
And I know that this may sound weird but
With the girl of my dreams, I just want to breath
The same air because my heart and my love for
The girl of my dreams is the kind of feeling that
No other girl could ever even begin to compare
To someone like her especially when I as a man am putting myself
Out there because there's too much love in my heart
F or me as a man not to forever declare because the
Realties of heartache and break are just too much for me
As a man to bare because I feel like I am the kind of
Man, who was assigned to your heart and your heart
Alone and I feel like I am the kind of man who could
Never leave you and your heart behind and as a man I will
More than care for you since I'm putting myself out
There for you and only you baby truly you man
Now and forever your big black teddy bear full of
So much love for you and only you

# The Confession Of Feelings

The confession of feelings goes even deeper
Than what even Ella Mai could ever convey
And the confession of feelings goes even deeper
Than what drake could ever say and is there even
A such thing as doing it wrong or is that just Marvin's
Room that a lot of us seem to be so damn stuck in and
Try even harder to get out of especially when there's a
Time limit to even escape such a reality but how can
You really if the clocks already been shot
And while you're still dealing with the confession
Of your own feelings there's something in you that
Telling you that this must be more than just
Some gut feeling that hurts more to show than to hide
Like a man and his pride along with everything
Thing that hurts him on the inside and his heart feels
Like it's about to break down like bad ceilings because
Of the weight of the confession of true feelings

# Bood Up

Bood up really got me so damn caught
In my feelings as I'm listening to Ella Mai
Hoping praying and wishing that I had a
Bae patiently waiting for cupids love arrows
To come over my way but still I remain sad
And lonely on this god given day because my
Heart mind and being Is forever being ignored
And so, all this pain from this emotionless reality
Is where all my love used to be stored because I
Guess that being bood up was just something that my
Bood up very soul couldn't even afford and so what can I
Really even move toward when all I feel is life's shade
Cutting and crucifying me with its unmerciful blade
And what I ask myself is when will a true bae love
On me and when Will I no longer be played as I long for the
When I can truly be bood up

# Will Love Ever Find Me

Now I can talk about my emotions until they
Begin to fade and I can talk to you about a man
Who has constantly been left rejected by the woman?
A man like him to be left forever played or maybe its
Just I am not enough of a man constantly being physically
Mentally emotionally and spiritually drained and tried
And with so many open and honest emotions it is so hard
To hide and I am so damn used to females hurting me that
It has damaged the core of who I once was and no amount
Of self-worth and pride could ever change that and I am is
Just a man who for a long time has been trying to find but
When will love ever find me as I continue to drown in this
Sea of utter misery thinking hoping wishing and praying
For any amount of love from any female to find a man
Like me because to my heart she has the key and still I'm
Looking forward to the day when love will find a man like me

# A Poem For Mama

Mama I thank you for who you are
And what you do and I thank you for
Being the woman that I needed for you
To be so that I could be the man that you
Needed to be for you and mama you know
That I love you and that I care for you mama
You are the most amazing woman that god could
Have ever made for me and I love that I am your
Son and that you are my mother and I am so glad
That I came into your life and that you came into
My life and mama you've always been the chief
Advocate in my life truly the driving force that
Is my being as a man and mama you've always?
Been there and mama I know that you love and care for me
And mama I now and forever love honor and adore you and above
Any other woman I will put you first and that will
Always be the case now and for all time mama this poem
And these words are all for you because you more
That this world to me and no matter what I will
Always go out of my way for you because you've
Always have gone out of your way for
Me and mama this is what I thought
You should know that poem for you
Comes from my heart and soul

# Anything You Want To Ask Of Me

I remember when my heart was only filled
With only vulnerability but you oh baby have
Shown me that from my own vulnerability I as
A man could finally be free to love someone like you
Unconditionally and all this love that I as a man
Have for you even blind eyes can see and anything that
You want of me I will more than give to you because
Your love and your love alone has and will always be there
F or me when I was going through and it was your
Love that held me down when I felt as though I was
Going to drown in life's grand sea but I have realized that
To my heart you have always had the key and that it will
Always have anything that you could ever want of me
Because only you could set this lonely and broken
Soul of mine free and therefore I will more than give
To you anything that you want of me as a man

# *Your Everything*

All I've ever wanted to be was your everything
Even sell my very soul and being to be your
Everything because I honestly thought and
Had believed that you could be my everything
And if I didn't have you, I'd have and be nothing
Because what is love if you have no one to share
It with and what is time if you have no one to spend
It with and what are dreams if they don't ever take flight
And what is being wrong if you couldn't ever be right
Can anyone just give me an answer? because I'm always
In this should have could have would have state of mind
And at this point in my life, I feel so lonely why won't someone
Just care for me and share my world and be everything that I
Would need for them to be and I could be everything that they
Would need a man like me to be I just want to know why
Things never seem to ever change and lonely was the heart
That has always remained the same and it feels as if it was
All just some game or maybe it's just me as a man who
Bare all of the blame because questions come up as will ever
Be worthy enough to be loved and will I ever be worthy to be
And black is the heart that surround's my
very soul and what more can I
Say other than I just want someone who
understands me and can be my
Everything so I can be those persons
everything because even in the mist
Of a heart that is cold you still can find warmth or should I say that
Belle who could be the love of your life and the only one for you
Because she could be the one in whom you
make your everything ebony

# Black Girls Rock

Look black girls are the type
Of girls in which you should never
Mock or gawk at because black girls
Rock and isn't it evident that black
Girls were heaven sent like each and
Every word that I've said I've meant because
About black girls because black girls you
Are awesome strong and know how to
Represent true blackness because your
Blackness has always been the highest of
All shades and as other races die out and
Catch fades because black girls no matter
What racial stone was ever thrown at
You today I will make it known that
Black girls rock in any time zone and
These are type of words of a seed that has
Already been sown and worthy is the inner
And outer complexion and tone that lies on a
Black woman's bone because black girls have
And always will rock and this something that
I as a black man have
Always known

# The Cure

Black woman I thank God for you
And every little thing that you do
And every little thing that you've given to me
As a black man I want to give back to you
Because black woman you are the cure to all
Of my heartache and pain and black woman you
Are the cure to what I once felt was endless rain
And black woman you are the cure
When I do not always feel like I can stand
And black woman you are the cure because
My very heart is in your hand and black woman
You are the cure when I feel sick in my very body
And feel like I cannot make it on my own and
You are the cure when I can't seem to find true
Shine because black woman you are this angel of
Mine and no matter what happens to
Me you will always be the cure

# Black Women

Black women you are the one thing that I as a man
Could never leave behind and black women you are
The one thing that always stays on my mind and beautiful
Black women you are who I will always want to make mine
Because black women I love the way that you walk talk and
Shine and I love why you as black women where even created
And I love how you as black women leave me so captivated
And I love who you as black women and how you are
Incredibly beautiful and more than amazing truly undeniable
In every way and black women, I love how you tug on these
heart strings of mine like guitars and I love the way that you
Even brighter than the heavens and all its stars
Because black women you are that light to a hopeless place
And you as black women can bring the realities of what love is
And what love could be into any real man's open space and this
Is why I will forever long for a black woman's embrace because?
Black women you are everything that I could ever want and
Ever hope to treasure and I love every little thing about you
And nothing in this whole world that we live in could ever measure
Up to being beautifully and wonderful made black women like you

# Your Black Is Beautiful

Black women I just want you to know that your black is beautiful
Along with the air that you breathe and when all I seen in this life
Was darkness you became my light and
because of that I as a black man
I will always have love for you to declare
and it will be your sins cuts

And scars that I will be more than happy
to bare because your black is
Beautiful and your melanin is what I treasure
and gives me the inspiration
To fight and because of that I as a black man
I will always have love for you to
Declare and all of your burdens worries
and struggles you can more than

Share with me because I want to be the
kind of man that can love protect
And defend you as black women with all
my might black women I just want
You to know that your black is beautiful
along with the air that you breathe
And no other woman in this would could
ever compare themselves to you

Because the flames of true love and passion
is what no other woman could
Ever ignite and because of that I as a black
man will always have love for you to

Declare and black women I am so in awe of
the beauty worth and honor that
All lies in your melanin realties that I cannot
help but stare and black women

You are the reason why I have these love
poems about you to even write
Black women I just want you to know that your
black is beautiful along with the air
The you breathe and to that place that is your
eternal cloud nine skies and chocolate
I want to go their black women I just want you
to know that your black is beautiful

Along with air and because of that I as a black man will
Always have love for you to declare

# Love And Understanding

Black women I as a black man know what kind
Of man that I want to be for you and that is a man
Who can give you all his love and understanding?
Because black women I need for you to be that
Someone that I can hold oh so close and love
On oh so wild because black women I am tired
Of feeling so lost as if I was a child without a home more
And I want and need to be loved and loved on by you
So that this loneliness of mine can all fade away
And black women you have always been on my heart
And always on my mind and day by day I grow
To love you even more because black women you
Take my breathe away and you leave me without
Words to say and so I am left speechless and in awe
Of you as black women and I am more than willing to
Show you who I am as a man and all that I can bring to your
Life along with the song that we could forever sing
If you just let me love you and show you my understanding
Because black women I want to know you heart and to be a man
Black women I as a black man know what kind
Hold and have the need to cherish you the way that I as a
Man can and black women from the bottom of my heart you
Will always be my something more

# This Side Of My Heart

To all the black women that I love cherish and adore
Worldwide all the love and passion that I have for you
Belongs to only you because I as a man would not have it
Any other way because black women it is you alone in
Whom I as a man would even consider to call someone
That is so close to me truly something so special while other
Women quickly fade away like buds in an ashtray and other women
Who could never be who you are could
never stay on this side of my
Heart? and black women I will never leave
you or your heart broken and
Rejected and I will never leave your heart unprotected because
You mean more than this whole world to me
a man like me and from this side
Of my heart I will always love you now
and forever because black women
You mean too much for me to ever let you go
and you will always have a place
On this side of my heart because my heart is more than open and
Ready for to now and forever be a part of it
all as my emotion's thoughts and
Endless feelings continue to run wild on this side of my heart

# Session 24 Pt 2

Black women I want you to know that
I love you from the bottom of this heart of mine
And that the love that I have for you will never change
Because I as a black man want and need you as black women to be
In my life because you mean more than this world
to me and anything that you could ever
Ask or want of me I would be more than happy
To do because your always in my head and always
In my heart and I cannot stress this enough because
What has been said has been said and this was
Something that I wanted you to know because
You're so beautiful to me and I wanted you to know that
You're so incredible to me and I never want to see the day
Where we would ever part because if that ever happened
Then how could I be a man that after your heart and because
I want you I do more than put up a fight and because I love you
You will always be that good thing in my sight and for you
I'm more than ready willing and able to be the kind of man that
You need me to be because black women
don't you know that you will
Always have a friend in a man like me ooh you will always have a
Friend in a man like me

# *I Just Want To Love You*

Look as a black man I'm saying this from the bottom
Of my heart and being when I say to you beautiful black
Women that I just want to love you forever because I just
Want to make these feelings and emotions that I have for
All of you to last forever because I as a man wanted and
Needed to put this out in the open because I thought
That this was something that you needed to know as
I cry out to you in the mist of my poetic and vulnerable
Sands while I continue to deal with my own and others
Emotional demands as far as this side of my heart now
Stands because all these emotions and feelings have
Truly taken over me because black women
I have realized that I truly
Have love for you but will you ever have love for me
Because I want and need someone who I as a man can
Call my own and all I ask myself is black women could
It be you because everything in me just want to be loved
On by you and everything in me wants to hold onto you now and
Forever even in the mist of these ongoing poetic sands and
Emotional demands within this lonely but open heart of mine and
Black women I just want to love on you
and to make what we have a
Forever thing

# The Only Women I See

Black women you are and have always been the
Only women that I see because black women you've
Always been everything that I've need and more and the
Only kind of women that I as a black man will ever adore
And my heart gives into you very commands because
Black women my life is in your hands and every part of
Me is what I will give you if that is what you as black women
Demand because I want to be your one special wish that makes
Your dreams come true because black women you are the only
Women that I see and, in my heart, I know that I belong to you
And that you belong to me and what greater love could be oh so
Sweet if it did not come from beautiful black melanin queens and
Women like you and you alone and if you and me both
Know this then you know black women that
Again, you will always be the only women that
These brown eyes of my could and will ever see

# This Lonely Heart Of Mine

I know you as black women and queens are truly
Beautiful in skin texture shape and overall design
And I know that you are so damn fine and I know
That only you can fill the void in this lonely heart
Of mine you were born so lonely and truly more
Then amazing and oh divine and the more incredible
And irreplaceable that you black women are to me makes you shine
Even more and everything in me as a man will forever
Adore because you are and will always be my one
And only and I just pray that I as a man never
Cross the line because black women I want and need you to
Fill this void in this heart of mine so that I can find
Rest in the mist of your endless paradise that is and
Will always be your everlasting love
Forevermore because black women I really
And truly love you

# Session 24

Look black women you should know that
I have been truly open and
Honest from the very door from what I have
been thinking too how I truly
Feel about you and the way that you shine
and I know that summer walker
Had her session 32 but for me this is session
twenty-four and since I am

Speaking from this open heart of mine black
women of you and your heart,
I want more and I need for you to be in my
life because you make every day
Feel like cloud nine look black women with
you I have been truly open and
Honest from the very door and to protect
defend and love you forever is what

I as a black man had swore and I will give
everything in this whole world up
Just to make you all mine and I know that
summer walker had her session 32
But for me this is session twenty-four and
black women it is to you that I give
All the praise honor and glory because I truly
adore you because black women your

More than incredible and amazing in all your
ways and design look black women
With you I have been truly open and honest
from the very door and black women

I will always profess my love for you loud
and proud as if it was a lion's roar
Because you need to know that you are god's
gift to me from heaven above truly

Divine and I know that summer walker had
her session 32 but for me this is
Session twenty-four and black women if you
stay in this life of mine greater
Things will be in store because no matter
how bad things in my life get if I
Have you then everything will be just fine
look black women with you I

Have been truly open and honest from the
very door and I know that summer
Walker had her session 32 but for me this is session twenty-four

# Bless Me With Your Wonder

Black women I love how you bless me
with your wonder and how its
My life that you enhance and with everything
in as a black man for your
Love heart and everything I will forever
fight and black women I appreciate
You always being there for me regardless of
my circumstance and no matter

What you say and do black women I just
want to see you win as you advance
In your journeys and paths in life because to
want what is best for you as black
Women feels right black women I love how
you bless me with your wonder
And how it's my life that you enhance and
for so long all I wanted was to be

A man after your heart and now I have the
chance and black women I see the
Value of who you are as women and why
you will always be my light
And black women I appreciate you always
being there for me regardless
Of my circumstance and black women, I
love that you never once looked

At me as a black man with a look of askance
and this is one of the reasons
Why I will always advocate and speak up for you with all my might
Black women I love how you bless me
with your wonder and how its

87

My life that you enhance and loving
honoring and respecting black man

Has always been the black woman's personal
stance and black women you
Are my sole inspiration for these love
poems about you in that I write
And black women I appreciate you always
being there for me regardless of
My circumstance and these love poems of
mines are the true stories of my love for


Black women and romance and black women
in the arms of your amazing
Endless love is where I want to be wrapped
tight black women I love how
You bless me with your wonder and how
its my life that you enhance and
Black women I appreciate you always being
there for me regardless of my

Circumstance

# The Greatest Thing About You

To me the greatest thing about you as
Black women is the way that you stand
Out and the way that you shine and the greatest
Thing about you as black women is that you were

Born with such dark chocolate skin highly melanted
Which all Is so damn beautiful elegant amazing and above
All brilliantly crafted and divine and with such beauty grace
And style black women you leave me as a black man captivated

And black women every time I think about you and write
About you in my poetry and its words grows increasingly
Invigorated and want for you all to know that black women I
Love you and that you are truly appreciated because I honestly

And truly believe that you created by God to be my everything
Ever since my beautiful brown eyes looked right into your
Beautiful brown eyes and had seen the
beauty of your dark chocolate
Skin and all its wonders that I love and will always have

Love for and black women I just want to thank you
Being all that god has and will ever make you to be and
That to me will in my eyes always be the greatest
Thing about you

# *There's Nothing More Beautiful Than*

I have never seen nor will I ever see any thing
More elegant or lovely in this lifetime when it
Comes to black women because there is nothing
More beautiful than black women because black women
Are beyond what true beauty standards and grace
Could ever begin to describe because the passions
Of my love for you alone black women
could fill any room with such
A warming vibe and what love and embrace could be
Any more beautiful and what greater woman could be
More than amazing when my eyes have seen any thing
More elegant in this lifetime of mine when it comes to
Black women because again there is nothing more beautiful
Then black women and their chocolate skin and the
Value and worth that is the black woman and that I as a man
Love damn much more because black women it's always been
About you because again there is nothing more beautiful than
Black women like you who are more
Than my dreams come true

# Life Has Brand New Meaning

Oh, black women I could not even begin to even wonder just what
life would be without you because black women as time goes
On and on I as a man only grow to love
you more and only you as black
Women could make this life of mine feel so
brand-new meaning and it took

For me as a man 24 years to understand this and finally get the clue
That your more than enough for me and
you make this heart of mine
Truly take flight and soar Oh, black
women I could not even begin to
Even wonder just what life would be
without you and if you were not

Around just who would I say black is
beautiful and more than enough to
When your blackness and the very beauty of your melanin magic is
All I could ever adore and only you as
black women could make this
Life of mine feel so brand new and you
true are the queens of my heart

And I will forever hold onto to your love
so tight like glue because black
Women you are my heaven on earth and my truly eternal open door
Oh, black women I could not even begin to even wonder just what
Life would be without you and I as a black man could not even go a

Day without you or your rich melanin
dew that nothing in this world

Or any life time could ever begin to touch
or even abhor and only you
As black women could make this life of
mine feel so brand new and my
Love and respect for you as black women
will never end and will be forever

Because to be a man after your heart is what I as a black man
Swore oh, black women I could not even begin to even wonder
Just what life would be without you and only you as black women
Could make this life of mine feel so brand new

# The Heart Of The Matter

To my beautiful melanin rich queens
The heart of the matter is that I have love for
You and I always will have love for you
No matter the cost no matter the hell no matter
The rains or floods or fires In all of that I will still
Love you because I need you and want you more than
I could want and need any other woman and I just want
F or you to know is that this is where I stand when it comes
To you because I love you so and you complete me with
Love so sweet corning right on in and changing me for the
Better and that is what is at the heart of the matter my love
And devotion to you and to anything that
you as melanin rich queens
Could ever do because my true feelings for you are
All I will ever confess and express and with nothing
Else left to address I hope the answer to being with a man
Like me for all eternity will now and forever be yes

# We Were So Meant To Be

Look black women it's my body and soul that you continue to heal
Deliver and set free and in the arms of your warmth and embrace
There is truly no place where I'd rather be and to the secret places
Of my heart black women, you have always had the key and black

Women without you being present and
making a difference in my life
There truly is no me and if you ever took
your love away my life would truly
Never be the same because black women
it has been and will always be
Your love that I'm trying to claim and black
women I love that you see the

Real me and the man in which I've became
whether I was in my highest
Or lowest of places of what I felt like was
living in shame and it is now at
This point in life where my once blind brown
eyes can see that black woman
What we have is strong and now I know
that we were so meant to be

And I have grown from a boy to a man and now I am saying this
Down on bended knee and black women ill forever cry out to you
Like boyz to men and jodeci and black women all I can be is me so
There is no time for me to run game when
a place in your heart is all I

Have ever wanted to truly claim and all
this love respect and admiration
For you is what nothing in this world could
ever tame nor the many possible
Realities that life presents before me because
I want to spark a new flame
And black women all I want you to do is
open your mind and say yes

To me because I want and need to be the
one black man that you will
Not second guess because I come to love
uplift and encourage along with
Taking away all your pain and stress because black women we were
So meant to be and that is all I will ever truly confess

# Amazingly Melanted

Black woman I love you because of who you are and why you were
Created and I love how God has allowed
for you and all your wonders to
Forever shine because black woman you are
beautiful and I love that you are so
Amazingly melanted and because of who you
are I as a black man feel so loved and so

Liberated and black woman you are the
definition of what it means for any
Being to be so divine black woman I love you
because of who you are and why you were
Created and black woman by you and you
alone am I as a black man left so
Captivated because your dark rich melanin
goodness is what keeps me in awe of

Your grand design because black woman you
are beautiful and I love that you are so
Amazingly melanted And I want you to know that
you are more than worthy to cherished
And celebrated because beautiful black
queens are more than enough when I
Needed a life line black woman I love you
because of who you are and why you were

Created and from your sweet love and
embraced I as a black man never want
To be separated from because kind of woman
that I want and need in my life is what

You always define because black woman you
are beautiful and I love that you are so
Amazingly melanted and black woman every bit
of the being that god has called you to be

Leaves me fascinated and black woman I as a black man am all
Your and you my melanin goddesses are all mine because woman
I love you because of who you are and why you were even created
Because black woman you are beautiful and I love that you are so

Amazingly melanted

# Brown Skin Brown Eyes

The greatest thing in this world is a black woman with beautiful
Brown skin and eyes because all that majestic melanin and all its
Wonders is truly eternal chocolate bliss and all I want to do is shine
My own light upon black women so that they can truly rise

And as a black man I just want to be the
answer to any black women's
Cries because black women you will
always have my heart and that is
What I will never dismiss the greatest thing in this world is a black
Woman with beautiful brown skin and
eyes and no other woman could

Ever be like you because there only angels
in disguise and any day without
Black women being in my life feels like
an eternal abyss and all I want
To do is shine my own light upon black
women so that they can truly rise
Because black women with you I as a black
man have formed so many close

Ties and in you I find so much love and
safety in your arms that I never
Could depart from all of this the greatest
thing in this world is a black
Woman with beautiful brown skin and
eyes and I love being in the mist
Of black women because I love my chocolate
highs and as these words

Of mine go on I enclosed these poetic like
love letters with my eternal kiss
And all I want to do is shine my own
light upon black women so that
They can truly rise and until time stands
still, I just want to be in and
Around your chocolate filled skies because
black women your all I'm yours
Now and forever
Ever thinking of as I begin to reminisce
the greatest thing in this world
A black woman with beautiful brown skin
and eyes and all I want to do is
Shine my own light upon black women so that they can truly rise

# Chocolate Skin Lover

To my chocolate skin lover, you have that
Radiance and glow like India Arie and the
Very God in you is what I as a black man
See and chocolate skin lover I choose you and
Only you because I never could choose any other
Woman because she could never be you nor have the
Same grace class and style like Erykah Badu because my
Chocolate skin lover your being alone is breathtaking and
All do anything for you all you have do is let me because
My chocolate skin lover I can be the man who can bring the
Sunshine into your life and wipe away all the tears that have
Ever been in your eyes because whatever your last relationship was
That could never be us because I'm a better man than the
Last man that you had been with and I want to be your open
Door and I want to be your something more because chocolate
Skin lover I just want to love you in only the way that I can as a
Real man

# I Could Love You Forever

Look black women if you me and my heart a there is no other
Woman's love chance I could love you forever because I know
And being that could ever be as that I can be the kind of man who
Can meets all Sweet as yours and no other
your needs but only if you

Let me into your heart woman's love could
ever make and into your life
I truly can be the kind of man me feel as complete as yours
Who can give you true satisfaction guaranteed and? and this black
Women is why whatever expectations that you have of a man I as

A I as a man could love you will more than exceed because
As a man that has forever because even before so much love for you
And truly cares for you I will I knew you
black women do all that you
Could ever ask of me and need of me I as a man had always

Because as a man black woman I could
love you forever so much love
For you because you are the only women
in this whole world that I and I
Always will could forever move toward
because my thoughts and inner
Emotions only long to protect and cherish
all of who you Are as black

Women and your very beings and it has
always? been that way even before
I knew you in this heart of mine is where
all my love emotions and feelings

For you as black women have been stored
and black women I only want see
You win and shine so just up open your heart to a man
Like me so that I could love you forever

# *Who Is Elijah Jones Love Is Action Vol. 1*

I know that love is real and that love is true and it
Only took 26 years for me to realize that all the love that I ever
Needed is what I found in you and in these lines of verse
Are only what black women like you could
have inspired because black women
You are who I've always admired and I love that there is an equal
Reciprocity and an unhidden generosity
between us and nothing could ever
Get in the way of what I feel for you or what
you feel for me and exclusively my
Heart is for you to keep and I think it's better
that it stays that way because this is
The way I know that what I feel for you is love
and this is the way that I know that
Your love rain to me is like honey molasses
and how you as black women move
Continues to show me more of you are and the way in which I move
As a black man is what you see when you're
watching me and as a brotha
I know that one is the magic and I know that
one day slowly surely, I will find
That one woman that will be all that I need
and more because the roots don't
Try to run deep they just do so you never have
to ask me if I remember because
Black women you know me like I know you

Oh, black women when I'm cold and I've dealt with all life
Has thrown at me and has its way of keeping me down its your
Love that warms me up and no other love
could do that quite like your
Love ever could and I'm not afraid to let the
whole world know this because the
Fact is black women I need you because black women without you
How could my life ever be golden and black women without you?
I'll never truly experience that spring
summer kind of feeling that I love
To feel and id figure id share how I felt
because these are the thoughts that
Continue to cross my mind and that's why
I want to talk to you and for you
To talk to me about what real love is and the
appreciation and understanding
That could make it the real thing with
powerful words and sounds when we
Both reciprocate it gives life new meaning
and black women I love that I
Can be so beautifully human with you and
I love that you can be beautifully
Human with me forever emotionally
transparent cause love is action

# More Than Just A Light Skin Girl

Girl don't you know that
You are so much more than a dark
Skin girl because your skin means
Everything to a man like me and it

Is all I could ever hope for and want
To see because I promise you that I
As a man will love you and your
Beautiful brown skin and all its blackness

And its highly embraced royalty should
Never have to hide because as a man I
Love and live to long for you and your
Very ebony shade and pride because you

Are more than just a light skin girl because
In my life the very light within you
Completely changed the emotional tide
In my life and from that point on all the

Love and the embrace that you've shown and
Have given I will never leave you or your light
Skin behind because your love alone has been
Oh, so kind and if I ever said something so

Stupid like your beautiful
For a light skin girl, I'd
Rather God cripple my very
and render my sight blind

Because if couldn't love you
Then why as a man should I
Even live or even see because
Your worth means everything

To me and so does your esteem
And that to me is more than
Words and a dream because I
Know that you are more than

Just a light skin girl

# Who Your Man Couldn't Be

Look I just want you to know
That I as a man more than love you
And that is more than clear to see and all
I want is to be all the man all that man
That your last man just could not be and give
You all the love respect honor that you as
A woman could ever want and need because I can
Be the kind of man who could provide it all to you
Because again I as a man I can be who your man
Could not be and show all this love of mine that
He could not be ever truly shown along with endless
Grace falling like raindrops because I want for
All the love that I want to give to you to reign down
On you and I want for my love for you and your love for me
To forever grow every day because of how I feel about
You is just all too real and with everything within the man in the
Man, in me and I just have to be
Who you man just couldn't be

# Let Me Hold Your Heart

Look black women I want for you to want a man like me so just let
Me hold your heart because I promise to
protect and hold it tight and
Never let it go nor leave it left denied because black women you are
The only beings that I've treasured like
this from the start from your

Chocolate melanin driven skin to who you are as black
Women true works art and I want for you
to know that my arms of endless
Love for you are open so wide look black
women I want for you to want
A man like me so just let me hold your heart because nothing me as

A black man wants to ever see you as black
Women part from me because I need all of you and
All of your love here right by my side because black
Women you are the only beings that I have treasured

Like this from the start and since I know that you are truly
Women after my own heart it is to you
that I dart because I just want
To run toward your unmatched love and do it all without my pride
Look black women I want you to want a man like me so just let me

Hold your heart because the woman in you is what is so sweet
And never could ever begin to grow tart and what I said is what
I meant and everything that you need from
me I will more than provide
Because black women you are the only beings that I have treasured

Like this from the start and since these words of mine of mine
Have said everything there is nothing left
to impart and black women
Before this poem ends, I want you to know that only you leave me
Satisfied look black women I want you to want a man like me so

Just let me hold your heart because black women you
Are the only beings that I have treasured
Like this from the start

Printed in the United States
by Baker & Taylor Publisher Services